Natural and cultural gems of Norway

Some of Norway's longest fjords, most impressive mountains, highest waterfalls, wildest coastlines, oldest stave churches and most beautiful valleys — chosen and compiled by Ann Waddicor and Erik Kjær Andersen.

...and where to find them

Introduction

It has been such an enjoyable experience to travel and explore Norway's varied and fascinating countryside, that we, an Englishwoman and a Dane, very much want to share our findings with other potential travellers.

Our travels took us around most of the central part of the country, everywhere looking for dramatic and beautiful settings and cultural objects that could be valued as "our" particular natural and cultural gems.

There's no doubt about it, the most majestic and exciting scenery is to be found in the west; with the long fjords, high mountains, enormous glaciers, impressive waterfalls, deep valleys (with up to one kilometre steep cliffs!), small farmhouses perched on tiny grass patches, and the wildest coastline one can imagine.

The eastern part has also a special charm of its own, with the huge forest of pine covered hills, long green valleys, big old farmhouses, large red-painted barns in undulating meadows; and towns with interesting architecture and museums.

It was not an easy task to choose among all our wonderful discoveries and make a selection for this book. We must emphasise the fact that the selection only expresses the writers' personal tastes; and, of course, that each gem presented here is only a fragment of an introduction to a much richer experience.

The weather in the west is less stable than in the east, and often cloudy, but what would mountains be without the magic of clouds? Sometimes curling around the tops like a halo, hanging like a hammock at a certain height; billowing like great ships; carded, as wool, up the rocky slopes, or just covering the hills from view, a grey glowing carpet of ferns, twisted birches and wild flowers lit up by an unseen northern sun. Here in summer the sun sets late in the evening.

The roads in Norway wind their way through the countryside, with hairpin bends up fjord cliffs, or across plateaus surrounded by mountains, through birch and pine forests, or along the edges of lakes. Coaches too manage the roads with clever drivers, swinging round the bends, giving you an armchair view. Most of the roads have a good surface, but some of the smaller roads, crossing the mountains are of hard beaten sand, with patches of holes and ruts. There are a network of footpaths, all the main routes are easy to follow as they are marked with a red painted "T" on stones or trees. The "T" stands for Den Norske Turistforening (the Norwegian rambling club). This club can supply maps and information in detail. Walking is one of the best ways of seeing into the heart of the countryside; hearing its stunning silences, smelling the bogs, bilberries and heather, seeing snow-topped mountains, glaciers, and blue reflecting fjords from airy positions. The mountaineering and trekking possibilities are innumerable.

On the by-roads one can come across summer farms and discover some of the old-fashioned methods of farming; here cows and sheep find havens around the tiny log seters, in a vast mountain heath Here too one can sometimes purchase unique specialities: the extraordinarily delicious sour cream (rømme), and the famous brown goat cheese (geitost). Norway is renowned for its fish, and for its cured hung pork and lamb, (skinke and fenalår). These meats are often used as party food, being savoured with flatbread, sour cream, beer and aquavit.

Apart from hotels, guest-houses, youth-hostels, and camp-sites with cabins or rooms to let, there are the special mountain cabins for hikers, run mostly by the above mentioned ramblers' club. Some of these cabins can supply you with ready-cooked meals, others are on a self-service basis. For these cabins a sheet sleeping-bag is required.

There still are a lot of wild animals to be seen, if you are lucky! Among the rare ones are: the lynx, the glutton, the brown bear, the wolf, the musk ox and the eagle. The most common big animals are the reindeer, moose and roe deer.

The Norwegians are a charming, hospitable, friendly, helpful and strongly individualistic people; proudly presenting their beautiful country. On special occasions they show off their elaborate national costumes, and play their unique folk music on an eight-stringed violin, the Hardingfela.

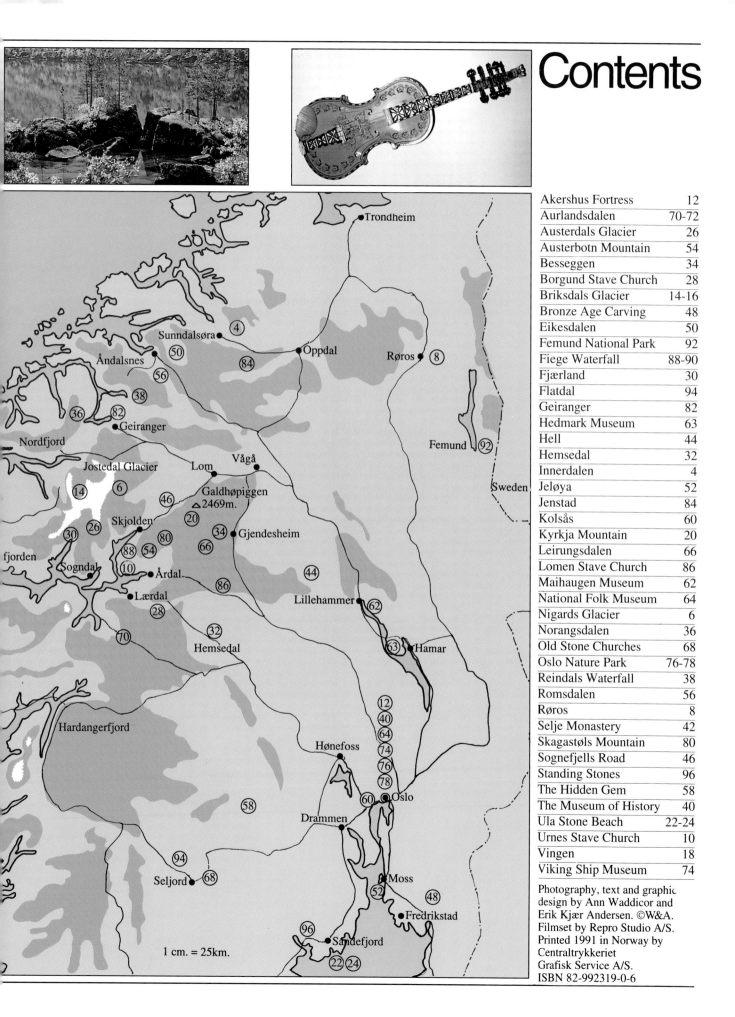

Contents

Trondheim
Innerdalen (4)
Sunndalsøra (50)
Åndalsnes (56)
(38)
(84) Oppdal
Røros (8)
(36) (82)
Geiranger
Nordfjord
Femund (92)
Jostedal Glacier
Lom
Vågå
Sweden
(14) (6)
Galdhøpiggen
(46)
△2469m.
(20)
Skjolden
(30) (26)
(34) Gjendesheim
(88) (54)
(66)
fjorden
(10)
Sogndal
Årdal
(44)
Lærdal
(86)
(28)
Lillehammer (62)
(70)
(32)
(63) Hamar
Hemsedal
(12)
Hardangerfjord
(40)
(64)
Hønefoss
(74)
(76)
(78)
(58)
(60) Oslo
Drammen
(94)
Seljord (68)
Moss
(52)
(48)
Fredrikstad
(96)
Sandefjord
1 cm. = 25km.
(22) (24)

Photography, text and graphic design by Ann Waddicor and Erik Kjær Andersen. ©W&A.
Filmset by Repro Studio A/S.
Printed 1991 in Norway by Centraltrykkeriet Grafisk Service A/S.
ISBN 82-992319-0-6

Innerdalen

Above. View of the "classical" shaped mountain: Dalatårnet. Easy to climb with a guide. Impressive panorama from the top.

Innerdalen is a mountain valley and is considered one of the most beautiful in the country. It is situated near the west coast, easy to reach from the town Sunndalsøra. There are about five kilometres to walk to reach huts, where one can get food and lodging. If you are lucky you might be served with freshly caught rainbow trout fried in local "rømme"sauce, and the choice of homemade foods. Innerdalen is a popular rock-climbing centre, with courses and guides; there are climbing routes of all grades. This valley is also a starting point for walks in the mountain area of Trollheimen.

Far left. Friendly, but shy sheep keep an eye on you, as you walk up the mountain.

Below. Looking west over the two lakes. The huts are on the right just out of the picture.

Above. Airy vista from the steep path to Innerdalstårnet, "the tower".

Above. The valley is extremely fertile with a great variety of flora; some of them rare; a natural rock garden that surpasses any we have ever seen.

Nigards Glacier

This impressive glacier is easily reached by ferry across a turquoise lake, but it is also possible to walk there along the shores. You don't have to be specially trained to experience the excitement of walking on the glacier, climbing ice-towers and exploring blue crevasses but never alone! Ask for a local guide at the ferry office, he will supply you with the necessary equipment and lead you safely up the glacier. Nigards glacier moves approximately 19 inches a day, making it sometimes calve at the bottom and therefore dangerous to go too near.

Top left. A child sees the glacier from a comfortable chair.
Top right. Ice roses tolerate the cold.

Above. At the foot of the glacier.

Far left. Nigards glacier wends its way down from the main glacier. *Left.* View of the Joste valley. The wide river turquoise against the white pebbled islands, rosebay willow herb along its banks.

Røros

8

Above. The church hidden
behind a slag heap.

Above. Solid timber walls keep
out the extreme cold of winter.

Røros has remarkable streets lined by old timber houses, much as they were when they were first built in 1644, at the time when the copper quarries were opened. Their enormous slag heaps are still a strange background to the town. Only a few places in the world have a place on UNESCO's list of protected towns or villages, Røros is among them, still lived in in spite of this being often the coldest place in Norway, with the lowest recorded temperature of minus 54 degrees centigrade! Its unique atmosphere is shared with the Femund National Park to the south of the town.

Urnes

10

Top. The simplicity and boldness of the older parts of the church, are woodwork art of the highest quality.

Above. The north wall.

Deep in the Sogne Fjord lies the oldest Stave Church in Norway, probably dating from the year 1050. It is listed among the worlds finest cultural objects. Particularly famous for its richly carved old doorway, its powerful beauty depicting Yggdrasil, the tree of life and fertility from the Norse myths. Later Christians banished it to the north wall to fend off evil spirits. The setting is one of the finest ever, on an isolated peninsular with a beautiful view. Urnes was until recently only accessible by boat from the pretty little village of Solvorn, near Sogndal.

Akershus Fortress

Akershus Castle, first named in 1308, lies prominently on a rise, beside the port of Oslo. With the Town Hall it gives the silhouette most connected with this city. It lies like a cat sunning itself, its warm-coloured gray stones a medieval memory, a fine facade to the many city buildings behind it. From here, once a seat of royalty, the cannons boom out their twelve gun salute, as important visitors sail up the Oslo fjord to the centre of the city. Now partly occupied by the army, cavalry

and royal guards, its cobbled streets still ring out with the sound of horses' hooves. Great iron doors, stone arched gateways and the ramparts, with their ancient cannons, all provide an enjoyable walk.

Briksdals Glacier

14

Above. The glacier slides down
between two rockwalls and into the
turquoise lake.

At the end of Nordfjord there is an extremely beautiful valley, leading up to Briksdal glacier; perhaps the most aesthetic ice fall in Norway. It is one of the many spurs of Jostedals glacier, the greatest mass of ice in Europe (490 sq.km.). Where the valley road becomes a track, you have the choice of walking about 25 minutes up to the glacier, or using one of the many Norwegian ponies and carts, which will give you the opportunity of taking part in an old romantic tourist tradition from the last century.

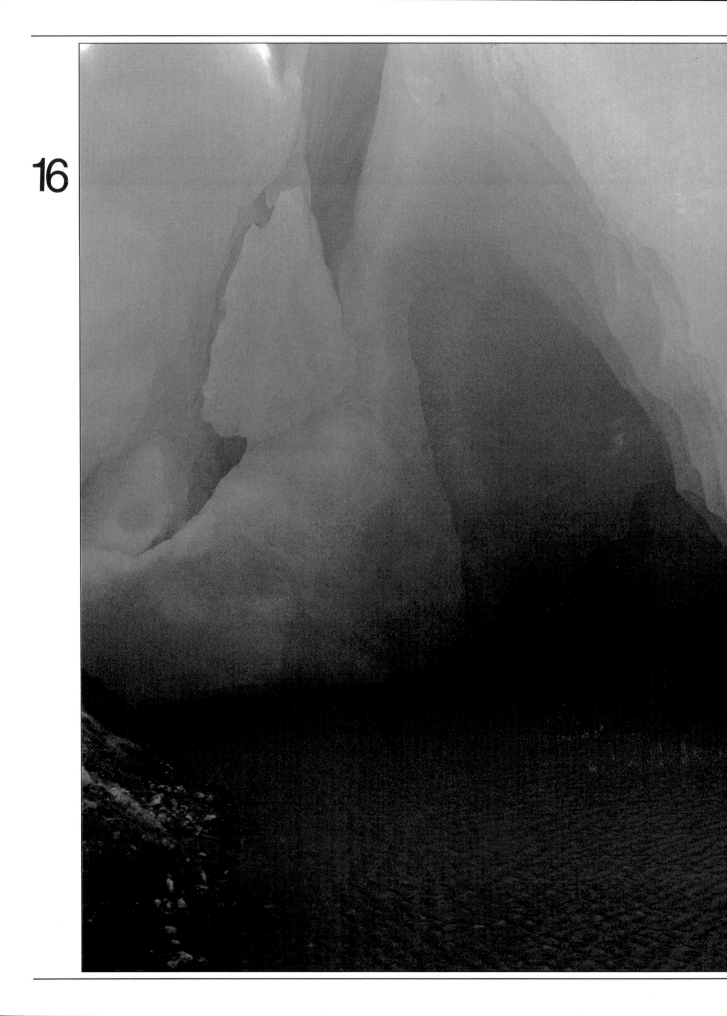

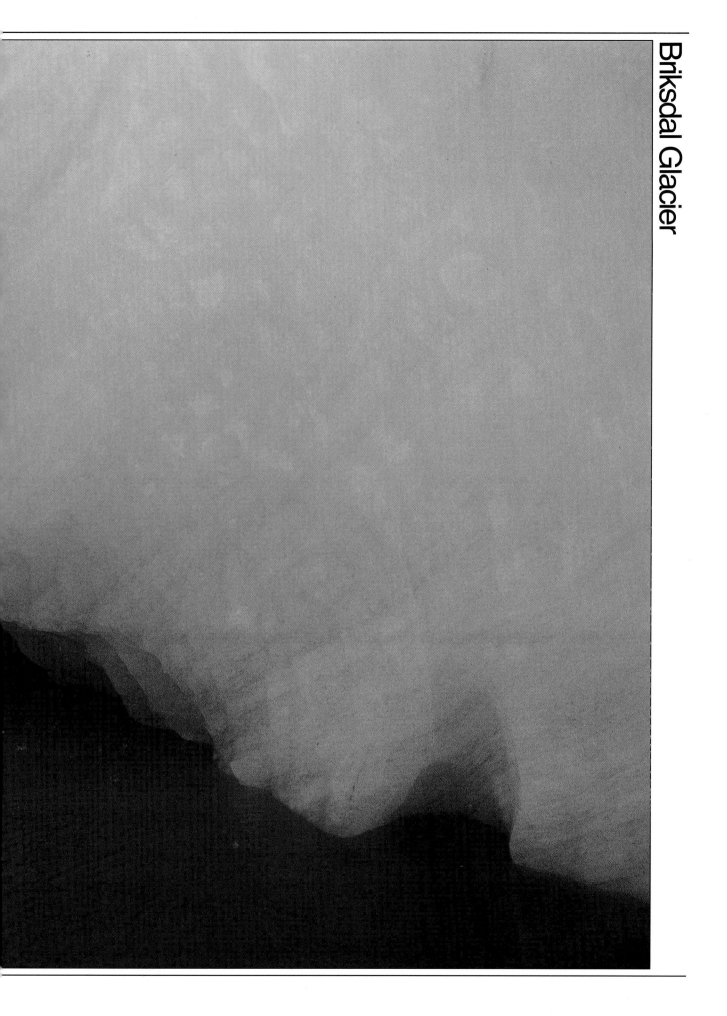

Vingen

Top left. Self-made "dolmen" with Hornelen in the background.

Top right. The river just before the waterfall.

Above. Such an idyllic place for an "art gallery"!

There are several enigmatic places where Ice Age art can be seen. The one that has the largest number of rock carvings is the mysterious Vingen, situated in an isolated, idyllic setting on the west coast. Opposite towers the highest rock face in Europe: Hornelen, 860 meters sheer drop to the sea! About two thousand carvings, mostly of deer, can be found on boulders and rock faces under the high cliffs. The carvings are approximately 6000 years old! There are two ways to reach Vingen, one by boat from Måløy and the other by walking from Svelgen. The walk implies camping one or two nights, and a steep climb up and down from the plateau. It is an extraordinarily beautiful, but strenuous walk, with a sheer descent of 500 metres beside the waterfall, and a constant view of Hornelens dramatic silhouette across the fjord. It is said that Old Erik: the devil, dances on the top of Hornelen on midsummer night!

Kyrkja

20

Kyrkja is a remarkable peak in Norway's highest mountain range, Jotunheimen, the home of the giants. The name Kyrkja means church, probably due to its steeple-like shape. It is a favourite mountain to climb, being one of the few that stands

Above. View from the top of Kyrkja showing the lake with Leirvassbu cabin on the far side.
Below. The path goes up the right shoulder.

alone, and because its fairly easy for those who are not afraid of heights! It takes about three hours to climb from Leirvassbu, the nearby cabin, which is a well established guesthouse type of cabin. From the top (2031 metres), you can enjoy a wide panorama of many of the most famous peaks of Jotunheimen, including the highest mountain in Norway: Galdhöpiggen.

Left. Surprised by snow fall in summer!
Top. Looking over towards Galdhøpiggen (2469 metres).
Centre. A cairn on the mountain road to Leirvassbu.
Above. The east side is a sheer wall to the valley.

Ula Strand 1

22

Ula is a sculptors paradise, an exciting place to explore. Several kilometres of fascinating coast-line; cliffs and boulders carved into smooth female shapes, here and there a kettle-hole, or series of kettle-holes; sandy beaches with milled pebbles and stones; stunted oaks and tall pines. There are many walks along narrow leafy paths among the trees and rock walls, or high up on the rounded domes of orange coloured rock. On the beach you come across big pieces of shipwrecked iron and wood from old galleons, aged into modern sculptures.

Ula is situated just a few kilometres south of Sandefjord.

Top left. A pink stone among all the beautiful pastel colours.
Centre. A warm coloured backcloth for sunbathers.
Below. A series of kettle-holes polished by the winter seas.
This page:
Left. A natural playground for children.

Ula Strand 2

Austerdals Glacier

Top. Waves of ice make a frozen
sea.
Centre. Below the glacier the water
makes the valley boggy and fertile.
Above. Midnight bonfire.

A dramatic eerie place leading up to "Valhalla" as the three upper glaciers are named: Odin, Thor and Loki, steeply falling to feed the beautiful tongue of Austerdals glacier. The relatively easy footpath in to the glacier, crossing many small streams among the boulders and low bushes, takes about two hours from the cabin Tungestølen. Those who are really tough and in very good physical condition can from here, with a guide, cross the big Jostedals glacier. If you arrive at Tungestølen on July 29th. you can join in the traditional celebration of "Olsok" — an amusing festivity with good food and dancing round a bonfire.

Above. A ring of stones marks the path to the old Norse Gods. Odin and Thor with Loki out of sight to the left.

Borgund Stave Church

This little wooden work of art stands as it did 900 years ago; the wood having lasted so long due to the climate, and to careful treatment with tar. Maybe it is this church that is the most special of all the Stave Churches in its wholeness. It never ceases to fascinate, even those who are not interested in architecture or art. Its character so impressed the Americans, that a copy was made and set up in South Dakota, USA.

Above. View of the church from the road.

Above. Dragons and crosses
protecting the church from evil
spirits.

Fjærland

30

The whole area is a natural and cultural gem: The picturesque villages, the beautiful Fjærland Fjord, the high mountains topped with glaciers, the rushing turquoise rivers, the many waterfalls, the charming old Mundal hotel, the quaint café at the foot of a wild icefall from Suppehelle glacier. If you are fond of walking, there is a steep path leading up to a small cabin: Flatbrehytta beside the glacier. It takes about 3 hours to the cabin, where the breath-taking view is a reward in itself. The most spectacular way to reach Mondal is by taking the ferry from Hella in the Sognefjord. For many years the end of Fjærland Fjord was an isolated valley, but since 1987 it has been possible to reach it through a tunnel from Kjøsnes Fjord.

Above. The reddest "eggs and bacon" flowers ever seen!
Right. This glacier once filled the whole valley. Cannon-like sounds herald new falls of ice.

Top. Fjærland Fjord seen from the path to the glacier.
Far left. The ice forms castle-like towers way up in the sky.
Centre. The old cabin of stones, with bunks inside, lies next to the newer cabin, where you can buy something to eat and drink, putting the money in the box.
Above. The path is steep but with a continuous view all the way to the valley.

Hemsedal

Hemsedal has it all! Beautiful mountains, rivers, waterfalls, woods; alpine centres for rock-climbing and ski-ing, several ski lifts, the most perfect ski and trekking terrain; plenty of fishing possibilities; hotels, cabins, cafes and specialist shops for ski-ing and climbing equipment.

Far left top. Skogshorn, famous training mountain for climbing. *Centre*. At the head of the valley is an impressive mountain, with a waterfall cast out on one side. *Bottom left*. Rjukandefossen (smoking waterfall) is the culmina-tion of several waterfalls.

Besseggen

34

Top right. Purple gentian.
Above. View of Besseggen, with
Bessvannet to the left and Gjende
to the right. Here Peer Gynt rode
over on a goats back!

robably the most popular ountain path in the country, ecause of its astonishing iews and "nerve-racking", ut easy climb, along a ridge etween the blue lake of Bessannet and the sheer drop down the beautiful turquoise lake of Gjende. Besseggen is also famous because the Norwegian writer Henrik Ibsen, used this dramatic setting in his play *Peer Gynt*. The walk begins at the tourist cabin Gjendesheim and ends up, 5 to 6 hours later, at the next cabin Memurubu. Here the ferry can take you back to Gjendesheim, or further into Jotunheimen to Gjendebu cabin at the end of the lake.

Top. View from the Besseggen towards the wave-shaped mountain Knutshø.
Above. Lake Gjende, its colour such a contrast to the blue sky.

Norangsdalen

36

Top. View of the Noranger fjord
from the path to Slogjen.
Centre. Slogjen from Øye village

The pioneer of Norwegian mountaineering W.C. Slingsby from Britain, said of the Sunnmøre area "I know of no mountain landscape in Norway, Switzerland or the Alps that can lay claim to greater beauty than that of Sunnmøre." He also called Slogjen, at the end of Norangsdalen, Norway's most beautiful mountain; it dominates the view from the top of the valley, a white peak in the blue skies. Norangsdalen has a wild untouched loneliness in its character, partly due to the sides being so steeply sloping, that seters must be built into the mountain-side, or beside big boulders, to avoid dangerous falls of stone and avalanches. One seter is drowned under the water, as a fall of rocks made the lake rise over its roof; remains of the walls can still be seen under the water. As you descend, the valley becomes narrower and narrower, darker and darker. In cloudy weather you get an eerie feeling, as the dramatic walls reach above you 1500 metres into the sky! At the end of the valley lies the little hamlet of Øye, with its charming old hotel, frequented by mountaineers since the last century.

Top right. Panorama westward from Slogjen.
Above. On the road to Øye; Slogjen in the background.

Top left. Old bridge from 1839.

Reindals Waterfall

38

From the end of the road where the footpath begins, there is an hours easy, but rather bumpy, walk along the banks of a lake. It takes you through a beautiful silver-birch wood with orchids, to a stunning wild waterfall. Reindalsfossen charges a long distance through the pine forest, before it finally cascades down to the lake. If you climb up the bank beside the water-fall, you get an unforgettable view of the whole scene. From here it is possible to continue your walk to a cabin, Reindals-hytta, well known for its home cooking and for the great old pine trees nearby.

Top. The path skirts the lake below the falls to the left.
Above left. A white buttercup.

Top. Reindals cabin fits in with the environment.
Left. You get butterflies in your stomach as you stand in the mosses at the edge of the rocks!

The Museum of History

40

In this museum is an ethnographic section with a fine collection of articles from many cultures, but it is the collection of old Norwegian objects we wish to emphasise, as many of them are real gems. There are the exceptionally beautiful axes and flint daggers from the Stone Age; many fine examples of decorative casting from the Bronze Age; and the medieval church embellishments, which comprise a particularly fine series of carved Stave Church doorways and religious figures. Not only is the Ål Stave Church doorway displayed (see right), but a section of the ceiling has been rebuilt into the museum.

Above. The Norwegian King
Olav Haraldsson (995 to 1030),
later made a Saint.

Selje Monastery

42

As the Norse Saga tells us, there was, in the 900's a young Christian princess from Ireland, who escaped by boat from the clutches of a Viking marauder. She and her followers drifted across the North Sea, and were wrecked in a storm on the little island of Selje. They sheltered in a cave, which later became their grave, blocked by a fall of rocks. The Christian King Olav found her with her golden hair intact, and declared her a saint; her name was Sunniva. Outside the cave, King Olav built Norway's first church. In 1100 the Benedictine Monastery of St. Albani was built below, which has now become a ruin, as have the several churches built there. The holy cave can still be seen high up in the hill, with a beautiful view out over the North Sea.

Right. The narrow entrance to the cave. The waters flowing from the source in the cave were said to have healing powers due to St. Sunniva.

Left. Harebells grow all over
Norway, the blue among the many
wild flowers of summer.

Left. View from the cave. At the top
of the picture a glimpse of Stadt,
the most western point of the
country, where the weather can be
tempestuous.
Above. Stained glass window
showing St. Sunniva in St. Olav's
Roman Catholic Church in Oslo.

Hell

A gigantic devil's cauldron is to
be found "in" Hell, one of the
most remarkable gorges of its
kind in Norway. There are
several kettle-holes of which
the biggest is 100 metres high
with a diameter of 40 metres!
The notice board at the entrance says in quaint English:
"The kettle-holes dug by the
river Vinstra at the end of the
last glacial period. The river
flew then out in Mjøsa [big
lake] 8 kilometres south of
Lillehammer, about 9000 years
ago. Vinstra broke through at
the Kamfossen waterfall 22
kilometres north of this place
and has since then had its way
down through Gudbrandsdalen"

Sognefjell Road

46

From the very end of Sogne-fjord, a road leads over the Jotunheimen mountain range to Vågåmo (100 Km.). It is the highest mountain pass in Norway (1440 m.). Before climbing from the deep valley of the fjord, the little town of Skjolden hangs, like a hammock between the hills, or so it looks from where Wittgenstein, the famous twentieth century philosopher had his cottage across the lake. The road starts to climb, almost literally, up the mountain side; at Berge we let Queen Wilhelmina of Holland, who rode over Sognefjell with sixteen horses, describe the view of Fortundalen below, as one of the most beautiful she had seen in Norway. The view is topped with the eternal glacier of Jostedal. Further up lies the old ramblers cabin, or residence, of Turtagrø, this is frequented by many climbers or walkers to visit the impressive mountain of Skagastøl called "The Big One" in their language, which can be seen to the south. Further up the air thins and is exhilarating, on clear days the view expands to all directions, a landscape of white topped mountains, glaciers and blue lakes. From now on the roads descends to Bøverdalen, passing several particular old farms, of which Bøvertun is the gem; in the vicinity are interesting grottoes. Lom and Vågåmo both have fine Stave Churches.

Above. There are many dramatic sights like this along the road.

Top. Old Turtagrø residence.

Above. Skjolden seen from the
ruins of Wittgenstein's cottage.

Bronze Age Art

Interesting Bronze Age art, in the form of stone carvings, are proliferous in the Østfold area. They were probably made by agricultural peoples about 3000 years ago, perhaps connected with a fertility cult. They are scattered about on farms and not so easy to find without detailed information; consult the local tourist office.

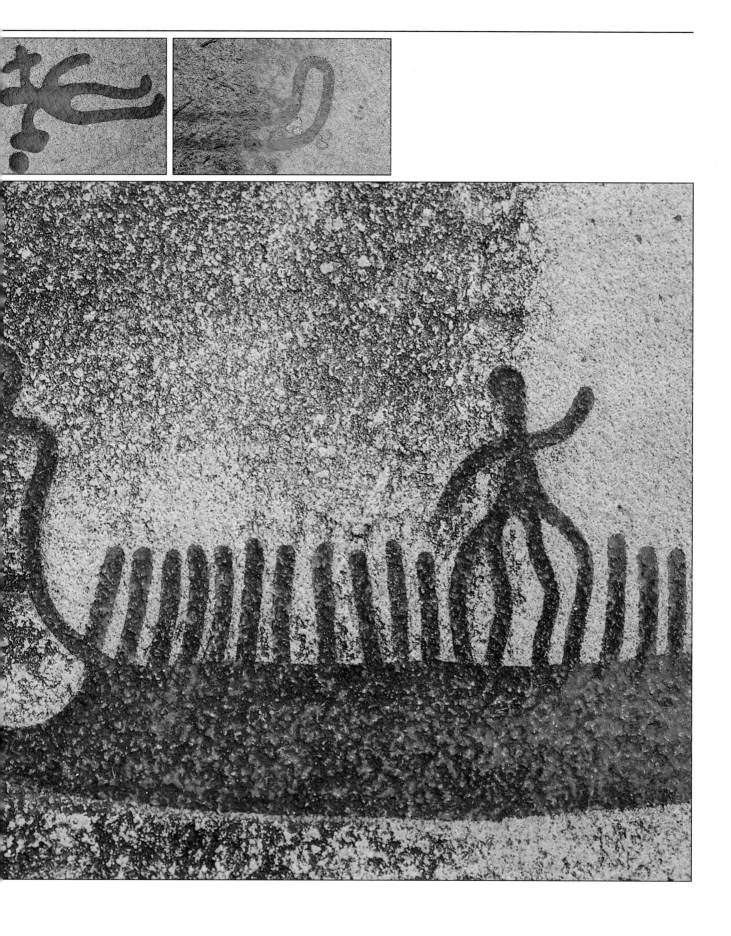

Eikesdal Water

50

Right. It is like standing in the first paradise of Northern climes, the big rocks with lichens, mosses and small flowers, or even a complete bonsai-like miniature garden.

At the end of Eikesdals Water is Europe's highest waterfall: Mardøla (297 metres of free fall). Unfortunately it can only be seen in July in all its splendour as, like many other waterfalls in Norway, it is regulated for hydro electric power. From Øverås, at the mouth of the valley, a ferry takes you 2 hours along the most splendid lake, with the impressive sight of sheer rock walls on both sides. The valley near the waterfall is extremely fertile, probably due to the high humidity and because it is protected by mountains from westerly winds.

Above. The whole of Mardøla waterfall, the upper part being the sheer fall of water.

Jeløya

South of Oslo there is the small town of Moss, and just outside it a beautiful island, Jeløya. A long avenue of trees with meadows on either side, leads you through an old estate to a white wooden country house, with great trees on one side and an apple orchard on the other. this country house, with its til stoves and big light rooms, international art exhibitions are held. It is the setting that make the visit interesting. To the north of the house, past the old farm houses, woods hide country walks that lead round the island, with small paths here and there down to the beaches Here stones, mostly rounded, are of beautiful smooth shape among the more rugged rocks the land.

Above. A grand old tree still clings to the beach like an octopus.

Top. Art Gallery F.15.

Centre. The ferry between Moss and Horten, decorates the skyline.

Above. On the western shoulder of
Austerbotn Mountain, the path is
easy this far.

Left. On the south shoulder looking
ast over Jotunheimen

One of the finest mountain
roads of Jotunheimen, narrow,
steep and winding; leads up to
Austerbotn Mountain, between
Årdal and Turtagrø. The high
plateau is a good starting place
for walks in the area. It is easy
to climb the mountain to a
certain height, where the views
are extensive, but to reach the
summit skilled climbing
experience is necessary.

Above. Camp below the mountain
with fresh drinking water.
Right. The flat stones made a good
fireplace, and a clear-toned
xylophone for the evening party.

Romsdalen

56

This is a valley of wild beauty, with great boulders growing mosses and small trees in the lush green of pastures, or in the rampaging torrents of the fast flowing river Rauma. If you approach from the east across the high flat moors of Lesja, suddenly the road and the river descend towards the wild valley of Romsdal. The mountain walls gradually get higher and higher until you wonder if its really possible; finally reaching its climax at the one kilometre high sheer rock face of Trollveggen! This wall is the tough climbers "paradise". There a number of other mountains in the area, relatively easy to climb, among them are The King, The Queen, The Bishop and perhaps the most famous landmark, Romsdals- horn. Near the end of the Romsdal is another valley going south, Isterdalen, on this route is a gem: Trollstigen, one of the most tortuous roads for vehicles to negotiate. It has eleven hairpin bends and a magnificent view from the valley to the Bishop and to the pinnacled horizon of Trollryggen.

Top. A airy seat on Trollgubben 1000 metres over Romsdalen.
Centre. At the start of the one kilometre climb, Trollveggen.
Above. Vengetindene.

Top left.. Romsdalshorn from
Vengedalen.
Top. An interesting museum in the
valley.

The Hidden Gem

Hidden in the wild boggy forests of Ble mountain is a little known gorge, with an unusual landscape of terraced platforms, idyllic lakes and rushing torrents through narrow passages. It doesn't resemble any other gorge we have ever seen, it is so dark and deep, that a photograph cannot give you any idea of it; you must stand there to get the full effect of its drama and all its aesthetic qualities. The river Gjuva flows through the gorge and out into Numedal Valley; to find this place you must get information in Flesberg.

Kolsås

60

Kolsås cliff, just outside Oslo, is a classified gem for climbers, with all its grades of climb and varied routes. Not only is Kolsås a playground for climbers, but for all who love nature and like walking up steep but easy, well trodden paths. At the top one stands as on the prow of a ship, with a commanding view over western Oslo; the fjords stretching away to the far distance. Underneath you, unseen, are the many climbers, like spiders on the rock face. Kolsås has a long climbing-history. Among those who have climbed here are many of the worlds most famous rock-climbers.

Below. "Gårdsplassen", a wide shelf or platform, where climbers have their gear, drink their tea and boast about their conquests.

Maihaugen Museum

Norway's oldest outdoor museum: "De Sandvigske Samlinger" at Lillehammer, is one of the finest examples of the many about the country; these can be found both in towns and villages. Each of these museums has a character of its own, according to the building customs of the area; it is a fascinating way of stepping into Norway's past. Anders Sandvig was the collector at Maihaugen, he wanted to recreate a collection of homes where one could go in and see people living as they had in the past, doing their various duties and making their crafts; showing their lifestyle and tastes, a mirror of social and cultural history. A special feature of this museum is its comprehensive indoor collection of handicraft workshops, fully equipped with the original tools and artifacts.

Hedmark Museum

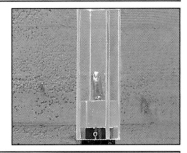

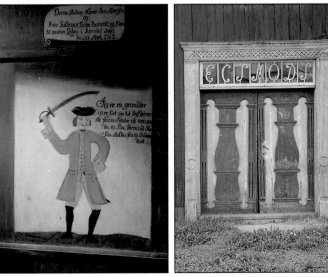

About sixty kilometres south of Lillehammer, beside the big lake Mjøsa, lies Hedmark Museum in Hamar. The most striking landmark of this museum is a row of arches, the remains of a medieval cathedral. Articles excavated from the ruins are housed in the Storhamar-låven (big barn), the stone-work is left unchanged and glass sheets are used in an ingenious manner; the whole creating a particular architecture which has been admired both at home and abroad. With its cells, corridors, flying gangways and court-yards it makes for an unusual adventure. The strangest item displayed their is "The Devil's Finger"!
The monastery garden fills the air with the scent of hundred and fifty herbs.

National Folk Museum

The farm yard, *Bygdetun*, was an important place for the whole community, a big tree was, and still is, grown there as a landmark and symbol of life. Oslo has a fine collection of *Bygdetun* on Bygdøy, part of the Norsk Folkemuseum, where buildings from different valleys are displayed in a natural setting; sheep, horses and goats graze the meadows, food is served in the farms, handicrafts made and sold in the houses, sweets and more in the shops. Folk music and dancing can regularly be seen in the summer months, where the impelling magic sound of the *hardingfela* violin, is heard, as well as the *langleik* harp and birch horn. This music and dancing can be seen at annual *Kappleik* festivals about the country.

Top. Detailed embroidery on the Telemark national costume.
Above. Some of the most bold and impressive buildings are to be found in the Setesdal bygdetun.

Below. The unique character, the massive boldness and simplicity of this Setesdal interior, can be said to surpass the finest interiors of the world.

Leirungsdalen

A wild, isolated, high mountai[n] valley, with glaciers, rushing rivers and impressive summits[.] Leirungsdalen is only accessib[le] by foot. It takes about nine hours to walk through the vall[ey] from the Gjendesheim cabin t[o] the next cabin Torfinnsbu; a strenuous walk, but well worth every minute of the effort.

Top left. Detour to one of the summits.
Above. View to the east.

Above. Take part in the aesthetic drama of Jotunheimen, the mountains of the giants.

Old Stone Churches

Above. Fiskum Church; the other pictures from Kviteseid church.

Top. Detail of a loft in a collection of fine old buildings in the grounds of Kviteseid Church.

Below. A black wooden side-door at Kviteseid.

In Norway in the middle-ages, when the most used material for building was wood, stone buildings were rare; perhaps it was used for some churches to express a stronger emotion than that of a mere dwelling. These stone churches have a simplicity of shape, derived from the Anglo-Saxon churches of Ireland and the British Isles, from whence came the beginnings of the Christian religion to Norway. These white-washed buildings, are only embellished by sturdy elegant porches, or small flourishes over the arches of windows and doorways. Their unusual use of a half-rounded altar wall, an aesthetic addition to the basic form cannot fail to move those who enjoy architecture at its best. Inside the same restrained style is retained, the white walls, the wooden vaulted ceiling, the pews with carved doors and the frescoes.

Below left. From the new road a glimpse of the end of the valley, just down to the right is where the path ends, about 12 kilometres from Aurland.

Below. The old farm Sinjarheim is now built up again much as it was before.

The valley of Aurland, first made famous by the paintings of Johannes Flintoe in 1819, has since become Norway's classic walk of natural beauty. The route usually starts at Finse railway station. The walk to the first cabin: Geiterygghytta takes about 5 hours. The next cabin: Steinbergdalshytta takes 3 hours. To the last cabin: Øvstebø 4 hours, and finally 6 hours to the village Vassbygdi near Sognefjorden. The last lap is by far the most beautiful. A particularly exciting natural phenomenon is the grotto: Vetla Hell, with it's mysterious lake. There are many waterfalls, rapids, moss covered boulders, deep gorges, narrow paths and the once abandoned farmstead: Sinjarheim, making the path colourful and varied.

Above. The little timber cabin shelters under an enormous boulder; no avalanche can fall on

Left. The river picks its way among the boulders polishing stones here and there or foaming among small rocks.

Viking Ships

The notorious Vikings built some of the worlds most beautiful ships. Their aesthetic simplicity of form gives one an experience of awe. The craftsmanship of these remarkable shipbuilders is unrivalled to this day. Every detail is a gem! The Oseberg ship is from about the year 850; it was a "coffin" for a woman of high standing. With this ship, buried under an enormous barrow, were found, miraculously well preserved, tapestry weaving, food and drink, horses and dogs, every-

Top. The Gokstad Ship.
Above. Burial chamber

Photo. Oldsaksamlingen

ay clothes and utensils; but the
most impressive finds of all
were the bold, beautifully
carved wooden wagons, bed-
posts, sledges, and detailed
dragons heads. The Gogstad
ship is the largest Viking ship
found, manned by thirty-two
oars, such ships sailed through
all manner of seas, all over
Europe and even as far as the
Americas. These ships with
their treasures can be seen in a
museum on Bygdøy, Oslo. This
museum recreates echoes of
sound from a thousand years ago.

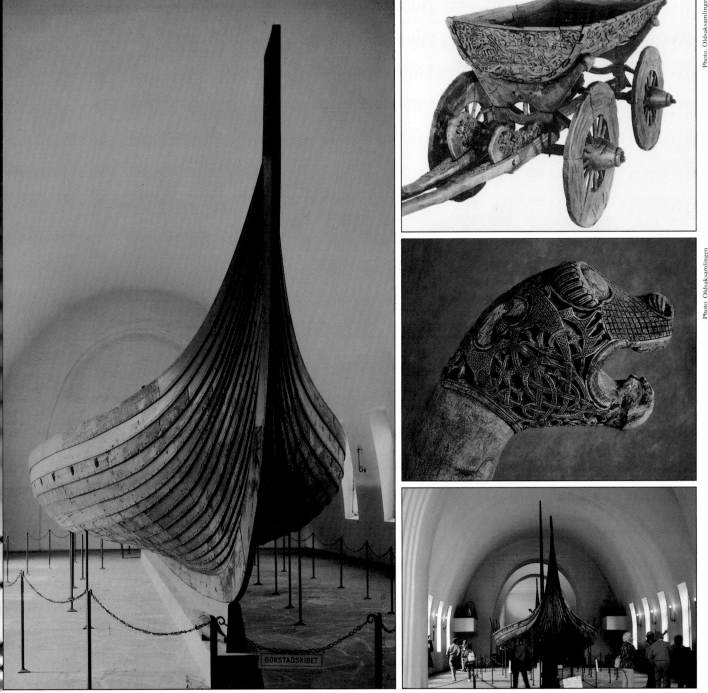

Above. The Gokstad Ship.

Above. The Oseberg Ship.

Around Oslo there is a broad green belt of wild countryside with woods, hills and lakes, which has nearly a thousand kilometres of marked footpaths and ski runs. Very few capital cities can boast of such recreational possibilities for its citizens. Those in the suburbs can literally walk from their doorstep more than 50 kilometres without meeting a main road, and sometimes without seeing other people. There are many beautiful places to visit - no wonder the Norwegians are passionate walkers and skiers, and at every opportunity get out in their beloved countryside!

Above. Looking over Oslo fjord
from Skaugum Hill.

Right. Hauktjern.

Top right. One of the big lakes
north of Oslo: Maridalsvannet.
Bottom right. There are as many ski
tracks as there are paths.

Oslo Nature Park 2

Centre. Hansak. The forest sometimes resembles a jungle.

Bottom left. There are many picnic places with natural shelter.

Bottom right. In all the gorges are moss-covered boulders, often with gurgling streams underneath.

Top right. An island on lake Maridal.

Above. The trees take on strange shapes in the snow.

Skagastøl Mountain

80

Top left. Every now and then a strange crashing sound startles the silence, as part of the glacier crumbles in a waterfall of ice, to form floating platforms in the lake.

Above left. Take a stick with you, unless you have an ice axe, as the snow can be steep and slippery!

Above. View over Midtmaradalen . *Top above*. Sundown just before turning in for the night, a reward after a hard days climbing.

Below right. A wintery world in the middle of summer—much snow fell the year this photograph was taken.

Left. The climb from the cabin to the top is lofty in the extreme and has to be acheived with ropes and climbing gear.

tore Skagastølstind is the third ighest mountain in Norway 2405m.) and one of the most opular for climbers. The mous English climber Villiam C. Slingsby was the rst to conquer this stately nountain in 1876. If you are not climber, the path to the 1500 etre high shoulder, between tore Skagastølstind and the earest mountain, is a real gem!

Through the cotton grass heath, past waterfalls, steep snow banks, two beautiful lakes with floating ice, and across a glacier, you reach the shoulder, where the sudden view of the other side takes your breath away. Just over the top a small stone cabin is waiting for you, with facilities for making tea, and if it is not occupied, a bunk for the night.

Geiranger

Left. The gorge-like walls are green with vegetation in every crack.
Below. The Seven Sisters waterfall.

If you approach Geiranger from the north, a wide mountain valley ends, and suddenly, far below, a view of water appears; one wishes one had wings to fly out over the little wood, and soar to the waterfalls and crags jutting out below. The woods reach to the edge of the fjord, with all manner of wild flowers growing on small meadows or stoney beaches on its shores. We have to say it: this is the most famous place of natural beauty in Norway, and we agree that the scenery deserves this label. In whatever weather, its magic of contrast is particular; snow on the mountains, dark sheer walls of rock, the blue or grey-blue water, the wooden houses with blossoming trees, the great ships, dwarfed by the landscape, bringing guests from all over the world.

Jenstad

Where the four rivers meet in a wild dance of waterfalls you find the deep gorges of Jenstad. Its an exciting place with terraced meadows, very old timber farms and seters, and a narrow winding country road up to the guesthouse farm of Jenstad. From here you have an impressive view. Perhaps this area is best known for its rare wild flowers that thrive in the rich fertile soil and the humid atmosphere of the waterfalls.

Above. The old weather beaten seter has become a shelter for sheep.

Above. Svøu waterfall, 313 metres, seen from Jenstad farm; an impressive free-fall of 156 metres. With farms above, some of which date from the sixteenth century.

Lomen Stave Church

In the Middle-ages there were eight hundred Stave Churches, today there are only thirty two:

Borgund, Lærdal.
Eidsborg, Tokke.
Fantoft, Bergen.
Flesberg, Flesberg.
Fåvang, Ringebu.

Garmo, Lillehammer.
Gol, Oslo.
Grip, Kristiansund.
Hedal, Sør-Aurdal.
Heddal, Notodden.

Hegge, Østre Slidre.
Hol, Hol.
Holtålen, Trondhjem.
Hopperstad, Vik.
Hurum, Vang.

Stave Churches are the treasures of Norway and are, fortunately, now looked after as such. The churches have an aesthetic simplicity of shape, based on a square. The roof is borne by solid wooden pillars in the style of the stone Basilicas. The name stave describes the framework that holds the pillars together. Their craftsmanship, ornamentation and beauty are of the highest order. The many tiled wooden roofs, dragon gable ends protecting from evil spirits, the decorative doorways, some of them ornately carved with the greatest artistry; the carefully chosen stepping stones to enter by, remind one of the charm and care taken in building a Japanese tea house. Inside, although dark and cold, the atmosphere, enhanced by candles on the altar, must have created a special religious feeling. The pillars of wood hold the framework up with no iron nails, only wooden dowels. The ceilings and walls are often painted with decorations, or illustrated with Biblical stories, in some cases the painters becoming so inspired that they left no space unfilled. Their character and power are no less than the great churches of Europe, albeit having a more intimate atmosphere, being so small. The farms were spread out and people often had to travel quite some distance to church, by horse or by boat. In the year 1536 the churches became owned by the King. Sadly, this meant deterioration set in and many were lost, but those remaining can make one stand in wonder at their individual beauty in the forested, mountain landscape of Norway.

Høyjord, Anebu.
Kaupanger, Sogndal.
Kvernes, Averøy.
Lom, Lom.
Lomen, Vestre Slidre.

Nore, Nore.
Reili, Sør-Aurdal.
Ringebu, Ringebu.
Rollag, Rollag.
Rødven, Rauma.

Røldal, Odda.
Torpo, Ål.
Undredal, Aurland.

Feige Waterfall

A 293 metre high waterfall plunges down into a black cauldron, watering the grass and the moss covered rocks below, creating an intense green-ness; and rushing on through the little wood, past farmhouses, finally flowing out into the Sognefjord.

Deep in the Feige Valley, at 1300 meters, there was a gold mine in use in the eighteenth century. The path to the waterfall takes about half an hour from the road.

Above. Feigefossen seen from the end of the easy path. The next part is more boggy and stoney but well worth trying.

Left. Dog roses grow well in Norway, and the cranesbill is common in the meadows.

Below. As you approach the waterfall, you feel dwarfed by the scene.

Above. The old stone-roofed farmhouse beneath the waterfall.

Top. Rock heather and lichen form beautiful carpets underfoot.

Centre. A mossy beach sets the stage at the entrance to Femund National Park.

Above left. Trees and rocks compete for a place on the shores of lake Femund as the sunset lights up their edges and the lake glows apricot.

Above right. Through this gap in the mountains walked early pilgrims, on their way to Nidaros Cathedral in Trondheim.

The wilderness of Femund is very unusual compared with other Norwegian National Parks, it has an extraordinary atmosphere of its own which cannot be described, it has to be experienced. The area is characterised by the wide views of forests, lakes and mountains. The wilderness, with all its interesting walks, lies round the 62 km. long Femundsjøen, the next largest lake in Norway. Nearby is the ancient protected forest of Gutulia, which has pine trees as old as 500 years! Norway's southernmost Lapp colony is to be found here. If you are lucky, you might see a herd of reindeer.

Left. This seter is much as it was in the past, cows and sheep graze, and the old equipment hangs on its walls; it makes a comfortable place to picnic, not far from the river.

Above. In this sweep of valley ice floated on the lake in the middle of summer.

Above. Ancient pines in Gutulia Forest stand or lie as they fall, grey white against the green of the surrounding trees and lichen.

Flatdal

94

Trees are tall in this flat valley as the sun sets behind the twenty kilometre long Skorve mountain (1364 m.); its steep side with small rushing waterfalls, like witches hair. In the summer it is a fertile paradise, a carpet of colours creating an ever changing patchwork. Small sheds and barns dot the fields and there is a village, unusual in today's Norway, with its cluster of farmhouses, stabburs, vegetable gardens and orchards. The deep gorges of this area are roamed by lynx, beaver, moose, roe-deer, fox and eagle; trees cling to the rock walls. The north end of the valley is dominated by Bindingsnuten, claimed to be the world's most painted moun-tain after Fujiama in Japan. Its shape inspired painters as does the particular lighting that again, due to the sun's angle, becomes magic to artists, the blue-purple suffusing all, the intense greens of summer and the reds of autumn. Many well known artists and craftsmen of Norway have lived, and do live here.

Standing Stones

The Megalithic culture (Stonehenge, Carnac etc., 4 - 6000 years old) has its most northern manifestation in Scandinavia. Whether these menhirs at Isterhagen originate from that period, or from a later date, is not possible to say. There are five stone groups, three round and two in the form of a ship. They give us a concrete link to our forefathers, creating a mysterious timeless atmosphere.